HOW DOES HEAT MOVE?

ALICIA Z. KLEPEIS

Cavendish Square
New York

Published in 2019 by Cavendish Square Publishing, LLC
243 5th Avenue, Suite 136, New York, NY 10016

Copyright © 2019 by Cavendish Square Publishing, LLC

First Edition

No part of this publication may be reproduced, stored in a retrieval system, or transmitted in any form or by any means–electronic, mechanical, photocopying, recording, or otherwise–without the prior permission of the copyright owner. Request for permission should be addressed to Permissions, Cavendish Square Publishing, 243 5th Avenue, Suite 136, New York, NY 10016. Tel (877) 980-4450; fax (877) 980-4454.

Website: cavendishsq.com

This publication represents the opinions and views of the author based on his or her personal experience, knowledge, and research. The information in this book serves as a general guide only. The author and publisher have used their best efforts in preparing this book and disclaim liability rising directly or indirectly from the use and application of this book.

All websites were available and accurate when this book was sent to press.

Library of Congress Cataloging-in-Publication Data

Names: Klepeis, Alicia, 1971- author.
Title: How Does Heat Move? / Alicia Z. Klepeis.
Description: First edition. | New York : Cavendish Square, [2019] |
Series: How Does It Move? Forces and Motion | Includes bibliographical references and index.
Identifiers: LCCN 2017059659 (print) | LCCN 2017060089 (ebook) |
ISBN 9781502637789 (ebook) | ISBN 9781502637758 (library bound) |
ISBN 9781502637765 (pbk.) | ISBN 9781502637772 (6 pack)
Subjects: LCSH: Thermodynamics--Juvenile literature. | Heat--Juvenile literature.
Classification: LCC QC256 (ebook) | LCC QC256 .K574 2019 (print) | DDC 536/.7--dc23
LC record available at https://lccn.loc.gov/2017059659

Editorial Director: David McNamara
Editor: Meghan Lamb
Copy Editor: Michele Suchomel–Casey
Associate Art Director: Amy Greenan
Designer: Megan Mette
Production Coordinator: Karol Szymczuk
Photo Research: J8 Media

The photographs in this book are used by permission and through the courtesy of: Cover Photo Image/Shutterstock.com; p. 4 Snapphoto/E+/Getty Images; p. 6 (left to right) Nemeziya/Shutterstock.com, Showcake/Shutterstock.com, MilaRu/Shutterstock.com; p. 7 Fouad A. Saad/Shutterstock.com; p. 8 (left) PashaIgnatov/iStock.com, (right) Horiyan/Shutterstock.com; p. 10 Luciano Cosmo/Shutterstock.com; p. 12 Robert McLean/Alamy Stock Photo; p. 13 Isabel Pavia/Moment/Getty Images; p. 14 MicroOne/Shutterstock.com; p. 15 G. Hughstoneian/Shutterstock.com; p. 16 Fouad A. Saad/Shutterstock.com; p. 17 Sergii Tverdokhlibov/Shutterstock.com; p. 19 Soloviova Liudmyla/Shutterstock.com; p. 20 Ben Burgert/iStock/Thinkstock.com; p. 22 Alexander_P/Shutterstock.com; p. 24 Maria Symchych/Shutterstock.com; p. 25 Richard G Bingham II/Alamy Stock Photo; p. 27 SSPL/Getty Images.

Printed in the United States of America

CONTENTS

1 Understanding Heat 5

2 Why Heat Matters 11

3 Heat Discoveries 23

How Does It Move Quiz 28

Glossary 29

Find Out More 30

Index 31

About the Author 32

A boy holds a mug of hot cocoa. The mug warms his hands.

CHAPTER 1

UNDERSTANDING HEAT

A boy holds a mug of hot chocolate and feels his hands get warm. A girl sits on a beach and notices her skin warming up from the sun's rays. An adult warms up a pot of soup on the stove. All of these activities involve the movement of heat.

What is **heat**, actually? Heat is a form of energy. In order to understand heat, it's important to know about

matter. Everything around you is matter. Your cat Fluffy. The air you breathe. A glass of water.

All matter is made up of **molecules** and **atoms**. These tiny particles are too small to see with your eyes. But they definitely exist. And they move all the time.

The motion of these molecules and atoms creates heat. So heat is simply the energy that an object has because its molecules and atoms are continuously moving. When an object is cold, its molecules have little energy. They move slowly. When an object is hot, its molecules have lots of energy. They move quickly.

As the hot and cold molecules move back and forth, they bump into each other. When this happens, the hot

The air in the sky, a glass of water, and a Siberian cat are all made of matter.

6   *HOW DOES HEAT MOVE?*

molecules share some of their energy with the cold ones. The cold molecules start to move faster. But the hot ones slow down.

HEAT AND TEMPERATURE

When someone heats up a meal on the stove, the heat from the burner moves into the food. This causes

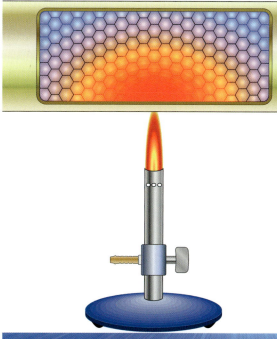

As the flame burns, the molecules get hot. This is convection.

the **temperature** of that food to rise. But heat and temperature are not the same thing. Heat is the total amount of energy held within an object. **Temperature** is the average value of the energy for the atoms and molecules in an object. We can also describe temperature as how hot or cold something is.

UNDERSTANDING HEAT 7

The bucket of water has more heat than the glass because it contains more molecules.

Let's think about heat in a glass of water and a bucket of water. The glass can have more temperature, or be hotter. But the bucket of cooler water has more heat. Why? The bucket contains more molecules and, therefore, more energy than the glass.

So what happens if you pour the glass of hotter water into the bucket? You might think that the resulting temperature would be the average of the two. But actually, the bucket has more heat. So its temperature will rise only slightly with the addition of the hotter glass of water.

HOW DOES HEAT MOVE?

The movement of heat is an important part of daily life. But how does heat actually move? There are three different ways: conduction, convection, and radiation. **Conduction** is when heat moves between objects that touch each other. One example of conduction is burning your feet when walking on hot sand. **Convection** is the transfer of heat through a **fluid** (like air or water). Ever feel a warm breeze on your cheek? That's convection. **Radiation** is different from conduction and convection. There doesn't need to be any contact between the heat source and the object being heated. This is how heat moves from the sun to Earth.

FAST FACT

Even if a mug of hot cocoa and a bathtub full of hot cocoa are the same temperature, the bathtub of cocoa has more heat. This is because the bathtub contains more molecules.

Heat travels from the sun to the Earth by radiation.

CHAPTER 2

WHY HEAT MATTERS

As we just learned, heat moves in three different ways: conduction, convection, and radiation. What do these movements look like in everyday life?

Perhaps it is a cold morning. Inside your house, the movement of heat (by convection) blows hot air from its source up to your bedroom. Your dad pours hot water

A pot of oatmeal cooks on the stove. Heat reaches the pot by conduction.

into cold oatmeal, and heat moves (by conduction) to warm up the oatmeal.

After school, you heat up a bagel in the toaster. This is an example of heat transfer by radiation. Before bed, you hop into a hot bath. The movement of heat (by conduction) is what causes your skin to warm up as the hot water surrounds you. Heat movement is everywhere!

MOLECULES AND MOTION— HEATING THINGS UP

Heat results from the movement of atoms and molecules. Sometimes these tiny particles vibrate back and forth. Other times they crash into each other. In solids (like an ice cube), the atoms and molecules are packed tightly together. They can only move by vibrating. In liquids, these tiny particles can vibrate. But they can also slide around or roll over one another. The atoms and molecules in gases move freely—and fast.

Heat is often transferred from one object to another. But why does heat move? It moves because

A boy soaks in the bath. The warm water heats up his skin by conduction.

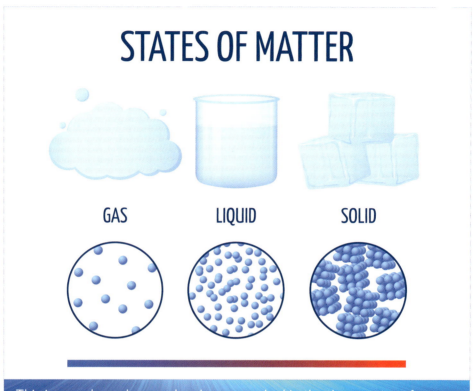

This image shows how molecules are packed in the three states of matter: gas, liquid, and solid.

there are differences in temperature between objects. Heat always moves from higher temperatures to lower temperatures.

At higher temperatures, molecules and atoms have more energy. They move quickly. When a fast-moving (hotter) molecule or atom bumps into a slower-moving (cooler) one, it passes some of its energy to the slower one. The speed of the slower-moving atom or molecule increases.

Let's learn more about the three ways that heat moves.

CONDUCTION

Have you ever touched the handle of a cooking pot only to find it was super hot? The handle was hot because of conduction. This is the kind of heat flow that occurs when things are actually touching.

An oven mitt protects the cook's hands from the hot oven.

The handle of a pot gets hot even though only the bottom of the pot is actually touching the burner. First, the heat from the burner

WHY HEAT MATTERS   15

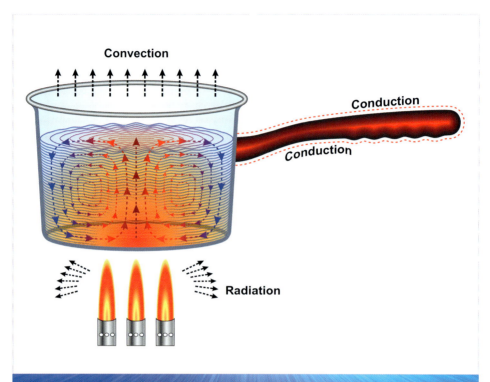

This diagram shows the three forms of heat transfer that occur when a pot is cooking over a flame.

causes the molecules in the bottom of the pot to start moving. Those molecules then bump into other molecules in the pot. The molecules keep bumping into each other until they reach the ones in the pot's handle. If someone touches the handle, it feels very hot.

FAST FACT

Many cooking pots have wooden handles. Wood is not a good conductor of heat so it doesn't transfer the heat well from the hot pot to the cook's hand.

The heat has traveled all the way from the burner to someone's hand by conduction.

CONVECTION

Convection is a form of heat transfer that occurs in both liquids and gases. Let's look at another example from your kitchen.

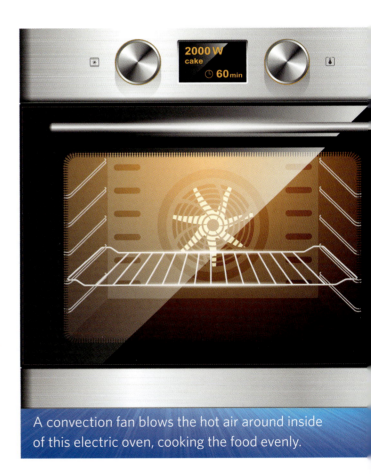

A convection fan blows the hot air around inside of this electric oven, cooking the food evenly.

WHY HEAT MATTERS   17

An adult turns on the oven. This oven has its heat coils at the bottom. As the coils get hotter, they cause the air molecules at the bottom of the oven to move in a circular pattern. The molecules in the air spread apart. The heated air becomes less **dense** and rises up. The air continues to rise and cool as it moves away from the heat coils. The air rises until it comes into contact with air that has the same density.

Once the air has cooled enough, it becomes denser than the surrounding air. This cooler air falls back toward the bottom of the oven. The air then gets heated again by the heat coils. It begins to rise again. As warmer air

FAST FACT

Heat energy always moves from an area of higher temperature to an area of lower temperature. If you ever open the oven door when it's on, you'll notice that the hot air coming out warms up the surrounding cooler air.

rises and cooler air moves in to take its place, a circular pattern called a convection current is established.

RADIATION

Have you ever sat outside and felt the warmth of the sun? Heat from the sun travels to Earth by radiation.

This boy warms his hands by a campfire. The heat from the fire is transferred to him by radiation.

Radiation is the third way that heat moves. In this process, heat moves as energy waves. These energy waves—also known as **infrared** waves—bring heat from the sun (which is hotter) to Earth (which is cooler). When the sun's heat waves mix with Earth's cooler air, the molecules speed up. That's why the air around you feels warm.

Differences in temperature swirl the blue color around this glass of water.

MOLECULES IN ACTION

What You'll Need:

3 clear jars or glasses

masking tape

marker

water

food coloring

thermometer (if desired)

Directions

1. Label the jars as follows: Hot Water, Cold Water, and Room Temperature Water.

2. Fill each jar about three-quarters full. One should contain hot water (about 100°F or 37.7°C). Another will hold cold water (about 40°F or 4.4°C). And the third will contain room temperature water (about 72°F or 22.2°C). You can leave water out overnight to get it to room temperature. Get an adult to help pour the hot water.

3. Add a drop or two of food coloring to each of the jars. What happens over time?

Friction causes a fire to start when someone rubs sticks together.

CHAPTER 3

HEAT DISCOVERIES

Humans have both felt and used heat since their early days. Ancient people warmed their hands by a fire long before scientists had a name for "heat."

You may have seen someone rubbing two sticks together to make a fire. How does this work? When a person rubs two sticks together, that action creates friction. Friction is a force that acts between two objects

A boy pulls his sister over the grass in a wheelbarrow. Grass creates more friction than a paved surface would.

in contact with each other. It can occur between any kind of matter—solid, liquid, or gas. This force slows or stops the movement between the surfaces that are touching.

But friction can be useful. Friction creates heat.

THE CALORIC THEORY

For centuries, scientists around the world have tried to understand heat. They came up with many ideas about what caused heat and how it moved. In the eighteenth century, there was a widely accepted explanation known as the caloric theory. The word "caloric" stood for heat.

According to the theory, caloric was an imaginary fluid. This fluid had no weight. The idea was that caloric flowed from hotter to colder bodies. Scientists believed caloric couldn't be created or destroyed.

There was a problem with the caloric theory. It could not explain how friction could generate heat. To

Friction warms our hands as we rub them together.

HEAT DISCOVERIES

see how friction creates heat, try rubbing your hands together quickly. What happens? They feel warmer, right? This is a simple example of friction creating heat.

THE FUTURE OF HEAT

James Prescott Joule was just one of many scientists who improved our knowledge of heat. In the future, it is likely that scientists will learn more about heat. Perhaps you will even try some heat experiments. Can people design systems to heat their homes more efficiently? Will there be greener ways to use heat to run cars? Only time will tell what new heat discoveries await!

FAST FACT

There are many examples of friction in everyday life. Using the brakes in a car is one. Another is sharpening a pencil. Even making a skid mark on the ground with your bike tire demonstrates friction in action.

JAMES PRESCOTT JOULE

This portrait of James Joule was painted by artist John Collier.

James Prescott Joule (1818–1889) was an English scientist. He is famous for his many experiments related to heat. In his best-known experiment, he attached weights to pulleys and strings. These were connected to a paddle wheel inside a container of water. He raised the weights then slowly dropped them. As the weights fell, the paddle wheel started turning. This stirred up the water, causing friction that generated heat. The temperature of the water in the container increased.

Friction -> Heat -> Increase in Temperature

HOW DOES IT MOVE QUIZ

Question 1: What is the difference between heat and temperature?

Question 2: Which form of heat transfer involves heat moving between two objects that are directly touching each other?

Question 3: What is friction?

Answer 1: Heat is the total amount of energy held within an object. Temperature is the average value of the energy for the atoms and molecules in an object.

Answer 2: Conduction.

Answer 3: Friction is a force that acts between two objects in contact with each other. Friction makes it more difficult for things to move.

GLOSSARY

atom The most basic unit of a chemical element.

conduction Transfer of heat between two substances that are directly touching each other.

convection Transfer of heat by motion in a fluid where warmer portions rise and colder portions sink.

dense Describes a substance that has its parts crowded together.

fluid A substance that has no fixed shape; a gas or a liquid.

friction Force that slows the motion between two objects.

heat Energy from the movement of molecules, which may be transferred by convection, conduction, or radiation.

infrared A radiation wave people do not see but feel as heat.

matter Material that takes up space.

molecule The smallest particle of a substance.

radiation Transfer of heat in the form of waves.

temperature Degree of hotness or coldness in a substance.

FIND OUT MORE

BOOKS

Mahaney, Ian F. *Heat*. New York: Rosen Classroom, 2007.

Walker, Sally M. *Investigating Heat*. Minneapolis: Lerner Publications, 2011.

WEBSITES

Bill Nye the Science Guy S02E10 Heat

https://www.youtube.com/watch?v=d9okTx3PsYA

This video features many everyday examples of heat transfer, as well as gives ideas for heat transfer experiments kids can try at home.

Science for Kids: Heat Energy Video

https://www.youtube.com/watch?v=xGKg3TSO4v8

This video gives many examples of how heat moves in our homes, schools, and outdoors.

INDEX

Page numbers in **boldface** are illustrations.

air, 6, **6**, 9

atoms, 6–7, 12–15

caloric theory, 25

conduction, 9, 11–12, **12**, 15–17, **16**

convection, 7, 9, 11, **16**, **17**, 17–19

Earth, 9, **10**, 19–20

energy, 5–8, 14–15, 20

experiment, 21, 26–27

fluid, 9, 25

friction, **22**, 23–27, **24**, **25**

gas, 13, **14**, 17, 24

infrared, 20

Joule, James Prescott, 26–27, **27**

liquid, 13, **14**, 17, 24

matter, 6, **6**, **14**

molecules, 6–9, 12–16, **14**, 18, 20

radiation, 9, **10**, 11–12, **16**, **19**, 19–20

solids, 13, **14**, 24

sticks, **22**, 23

sun, 5, 9, **10**, 19–20

temperature, 7, 9, 14, 27

vibration, 12–13

ABOUT THE AUTHOR

Alicia Klepeis began her career as a writer at the National Geographic Society. She is the author of numerous children's books, including Trolls, Haunted Cemeteries Around the World, and A Time for Change. Alicia's favorite form of heat transfer is holding a cup of hot tea on a cold day.